HALOGEN OVEN COOKING

Lakeland and Octopus Publishing Group
Limited hereby exclude all liability to the
extent permitted by law for any errors or
omission in this book and for any loss,
damage or expense (whether direct or
indirect) suffered by a third party relying
on any information contained in this book.

This book was published in 2012 for
Lakeland by Hamlyn, a division of
Octopus Publishing Group Limited

Endeavour House
189 Shaftesbury Avenue
London WC2H 8JY
United Kingdom
phone +44 (0) 207 632 5400
fax +44 (0) 207 632 5405
www.octopusbooks.co.uk

Printed and bound in China

A catalogue record for this book is
available from the British Library.

This publication is copyright. No part of
it may be reproduced or transmitted in
any form without the written permission
of the Publisher.

ISBN 978-0-600-62563-6

© Octopus Publishing Group Limited 2012
Glossary text and endpaper image © ACP
Magazines Ltd 2012

The Department of Health advises that
eggs should not be consumed raw.
This book contains some dishes made
with raw or lightly cooked eggs. It is
prudent for vulnerable people such as
pregnant and nursing mothers, invalids,
the elderly, babies and young children to
avoid uncooked or lightly cooked dishes
made with eggs. Once prepared, these
dishes should be kept refrigerated and
used promptly.

This book also includes dishes made with
nuts and nut derivatives. It is advisable
for those with known allergic reactions to
nuts and nut derivatives and those who
may be potentially vulnerable to these
allergies, such as pregnant and nursing
mothers, invalids, the elderly, babies and
children to avoid dishes made with nuts
and nut oils. It is also prudent to check the
labels of pre-prepared ingredients for the
possible inclusion of nut derivatives.

Some of the recipes in this book have
appeared in other publications.

HALOGEN OVEN COOKING

Portable and compact, halogen ovens cook up to five times faster than conventional ovens and produce delicious results. Learn how to make the most of your halogen oven with this brilliant collection of 52 recipes for every occasion.

One of an exciting new series of cookbooks from Lakeland, *Halogen Oven Cooking* is packed with delicious colour photos and expert hints, tips and techniques for beginners and experienced cooks alike.

These excellent cookbooks are sure to be some of the best-loved on your kitchen bookshelf. To discover the rest of the range, together with our unrivalled selection of creative kitchenware, visit one of our friendly Lakeland stores or shop online at www.lakeland.co.uk.

CONTENTS

GETTING STARTED

Combining the convenience of a microwave oven with the benefits of a conventional oven, halogen ovens are ideal for the busy cook.

WHY CHOOSE HALOGEN?
• Cooking time is up to five times faster.
• Fat is drained away from meat cooked directly on the rack which makes for healthier eating.
• They're fan-assisted so food cooks evenly and quickly and is deliciously crisp and crunchy.

• They're compact too which makes them ideal for small kitchens and they're becoming a popular choice for caravanning holidays.
• There's no need to defrost – meat, fish and poultry can be cooked straight from the freezer.
• The glass bowl means you can easily see the progress of your dish – no more opening the oven door to see if your cake has risen!

HOW DOES IT WORK?
Halogen ovens use a combination of powerful halogen lighting and convection currents. The infrared halogen element heats up almost instantly, reducing the time the oven needs to preheat prior to cooking. To cook you have a choice: you can cook directly on the rack (or racks, if your oven has two); certain ingredients can be cooked inside the glass bowl itself; or you can place an ordinary cooking dish or roasting pan inside the oven to cook in much the same way as in a conventional oven.

YOUR HALOGEN OVEN
Halogen ovens are generally supplied with:
• glass bowl
• base stand
• lid with halogen element and power cord
• a steel rack; some halogen ovens come with two racks: an upper and a lower one
• steel handles for safe removal of the racks
• extender ring to raise the height of the lid to give extra room inside

For most ovens you can also buy a range of extra equipment and accessories such as steamer pans, frying pans and lid stands. You can also purchase a second rack for your oven, if it has only one.

It's a good idea to see what you use the halogen oven for most before deciding what else you might need to get to complement it. You can use your existing oven trays, casserole dishes, baking trays and so on, but do double-check that they will fit easily inside your halogen oven before beginning.

USING YOUR OVEN

Always follow the instructions in the manufacturer's manual that will come with your particular oven but generally they are set up in the following way:

• Place the glass bowl on the metal base and be sure to do so on a steady, flat and secure worktop or table near an electrical socket.

• The metal rack then sits inside the glass bowl. If you are using two metal racks, they fit in one on top of the other.

• Next fit the lid onto the glass bowl and push the handle down to lock it.

• Plug the oven into a nearby socket. Turn the timer dial to select the required cooking time. The power light will now be on.

• Turn the temperature dial to select the required temperature. The light will then come on. When the oven gets to the right temperature this light will go off.

• When the food is ready – which is normally indicated by the bell ringing – carefully remove it from the glass bowl using the steel handles.

CLEANING YOUR OVEN

The glass bowl can be placed in the dishwasher for cleaning or the bowl and rack can be cleaned using warm soapy water. If there is any burnt-on residue you might want to soak the bowl or rack in warm water. The lid should be kept clean by wiping it with a damp cloth. Never immerse the whole appliance in water.

WHAT TO COOK?

You can cook almost any food in your halogen oven, even toast! Halogen ovens can be used for steaming, baking, boiling, roasting, frying and grilling and most halogen ovens can cook frozen foods and some also have thaw functions. Make sure that you read the manufacturer's instructions for your particular model to check what foods are suitable for cooking in it.

COOKING TIMES

Most halogen ovens have a lowest temperature setting of around 125°C (275°F) and a highest setting of 250°C (482°F). You will notice that these are similar to the settings of a conventional oven. However, the design of the halogen oven means that cooking times are vastly reduced. By moving hot air rapidly around, a halogen oven cooks food evenly and quickly without hot and cold spots and this helps to shorten the time usually needed.

ABOUT THE RECIPES IN THIS BOOK

Preheating You will notice that the recipes in this book don't require you to preheat the oven. While halogen ovens can be preheated – most notably, for baking cakes or puddings – the cooking times for the recipes in this book have been adjusted so that preheating is unnecessary.

You simply assemble and prepare the ingredients as directed, put the food in the oven, fit and close the lid and set the timer and temperature dials.

Other cooking methods Some recipes do require part of the preparation to be done using the hob but the cooking methods needed are uncomplicated and designed to achieve the best finished dish while still making the most of your halogen oven.

MEAT

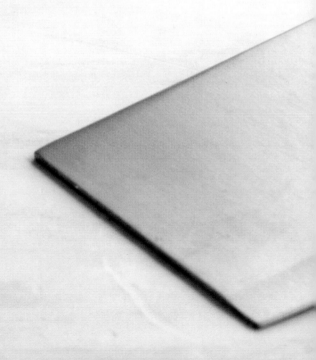

ROAST SIRLOIN OF BEEF

1.25 kg (2½ lb) piece of rolled
 sirloin of beef
2 large onions, sliced
several thyme sprigs
2 tablespoons olive oil
2 teaspoons plain flour
2 teaspoons dry mustard
200 ml (7 fl oz) red wine
salt and pepper

1 Rub the beef on all sides with plenty of salt and pepper. Scatter the onions and thyme sprigs in a roasting tin and rest the beef on top. Drizzle with the oil and place on the lower rack of the halogen oven.

2 Set the temperature to 225°C (437°F) and cook for 20 minutes, turning twice during cooking to seal and brown the meat. Mix together the flour and mustard powder. Turn the meat so that the fat side is uppermost and sprinkle with the flour mixture. Reduce the temperature to 175°C (347°F) and cook for a further 15–20 minutes. (The beef will still be pink in the centre, so cook for a little longer if you prefer beef cooked through.) Transfer the meat to a board or platter and leave to rest for 20 minutes before carving.

3 Skim any fat from the juices in the roasting tin and fry the onions for 10 minutes. Pour in the wine and cook for a further 5 minutes. Season to taste and strain into a gravy jug. Serve with the beef.

prep + cook time about 1 hour + resting time
serves 4–5

RICH BEEF STEW WITH TAPENADE

1 tablespoon plain flour
750 g (1½ lb) braising beef,
    cut into small pieces
3 tablespoons olive oil
1 large onion, chopped
3 carrots, sliced
4 garlic cloves, crushed
several pared strips of orange
    rind
several thyme sprigs
300 ml (½ pint) red wine
400 g (13 oz) can chopped
    tomatoes
4 tablespoons sun-dried
    tomato paste
1 tablespoon molasses or
    black treacle
5 tablespoons black olive
    tapenade
salt and pepper
polenta or pasta, to serve

1 Season the flour with salt and pepper and use it to coat the beef. Heat the oil in a frying pan on the hob and fry the meat, in batches, to brown, transferring the browned meat to a casserole dish. Add the onion and carrots to the pan and fry for 5 minutes to soften. Add the garlic and fry for a further 1 minute.

2 Add the orange rind, thyme, wine, tomatoes, tomato paste, molasses or treacle and a little seasoning to the pan and bring to the boil. Add the mixture to the casserole dish. Cover with foil and place the dish on the lower rack of the halogen oven.

3 Set the temperature to 175°C (347°F) and cook for 1½ hours or until the beef is tender. Stir in the tapenade and cook for a further 10 minutes. Check the seasoning and serve with creamy polenta or pasta.

prep + cook time about 2 hours
serves 4

BEEF & BARLEY STEW

450 g (14½ oz) lean braising
  steak, cut into chunks
4 carrots, sliced
2 leeks, sliced
300 g (10 oz) swede, cut into
  small chunks
100 g (3½ oz) pearl barley
1 bouquet garni
900 ml (1½ pints) beef stock
salt and pepper

1 Put the steak, carrots, leeks,
swede, pearl barley and bouquet
garni in a saucepan on the hob.
Add the stock and bring to a
gentle simmer.
2 Transfer the contents of the pan
to a casserole dish and cover with
foil. Place on the lower rack of the
halogen oven.
3 Set the temperature to 200°C
(392°F) and cook for 50–60 minutes,
stirring every 20 minutes, until the
meat is tender. Season to taste
with salt and pepper, and serve
with potato or celeriac mash and
green beans.

prep + cook time 1 hour
25 minutes
serves 4

CHILLI PEPPER BURGERS

450 g (14½ oz) lean minced beef
1 small onion, finely chopped
1 garlic clove, crushed
1 small red pepper, cored,
    deseeded and finely diced
½ teaspoon dried mixed herbs
2 tablespoons sweet chilli sauce
40g (1½ oz) fresh white
    breadcrumbs
1 egg, beaten
1 tablespoon sunflower or
    vegetable oil
salt and pepper

to serve
4 burger buns
handful of crisp lettuce leaves
tomato slices
red onion slices

1 Put the mince in a bowl and add the onion, garlic, red pepper, herbs, sweet chilli sauce and breadcrumbs. Add the egg and season with a little salt and pepper. Mix well. (This is best done with your hands.) Shape the mixture into 4 large burgers, and place on a baking sheet lined with nonstick baking paper. Cover loosely and chill for at least 30 minutes.
2 Brush each burger lightly with the oil and place on the upper rack of the halogen oven.
3 Set the temperature to 225°C (437°F) and grill the burgers for about 14 minutes, turning halfway through cooking, until cooked through. Serve in the burger buns with crisp lettuce leaves and tomato and onion slices, and accompany with mayonnaise and relish or pickle.

prep + cook time 30 minutes + chilling time
serves 4

ASIAN GINGER BEEF

3 tablespoons wok or stir-fry oil
700 g (1 lb 6 oz) lean braising
  steak, cut into small chunks
2 celery sticks, sliced
2 red peppers, cored, deseeded
  and cut into chunks
400 ml (14 fl oz) hot beef or
  vegetable stock
1 tablespoon dark soy sauce
3 cm (1¼ inch) piece of fresh root
  ginger, grated
½ teaspoon crushed dried red
  chillies
1 tablespoon cornflour
2 tablespoons water
200 g (7 oz) sugarsnap peas,
  halved lengthways
½ bunch of spring onions, sliced
Thai fragrant rice, to serve

1 Heat 2 tablespoons of the oil in a large frying pan on the hob and fry the beef, in batches, until lightly browned. Transfer to a casserole dish. Add the remaining oil to the pan and fry the celery and peppers until beginning to soften. Add to the dish.

2 Pour over the stock and add the soy sauce, ginger and chillies. Stir gently to mix. Cover with foil and place on the lower rack of the halogen oven.

3 Set the temperature to 200°C (392°F) and cook for 50 minutes or until the beef is tender. Blend the cornflour with the water. Stir into the beef and add the sugarsnap peas and spring onions. Cover and cook for a further 10 minutes. Serve with Thai fragrant rice.

prep + cook time 1 hour 35 minutes
serves 6

TRADITIONAL BEEF SATAY

½ bunch of spring onions, chopped

2.5 cm (1 inch) piece of fresh root ginger, chopped

2 garlic cloves, chopped

8 cardamom pods

1 teaspoon each cumin and coriander seeds, lightly crushed

4 tablespoons lemon juice

½ teaspoon freshly grated nutmeg

2 bay leaves, crumbled

2 tablespoons vegetable oil

700 g (1 lb 7 oz) rump steak, trimmed and cut into chunks

6 tablespoons peanut butter

1 tablespoon light muscovado sugar

1 red chilli, deseeded and chopped

2 tablespoons dark soy sauce

150 ml (¼ pint) beef stock

to serve
rice
lime quarters

1 Put the spring onions, ginger, garlic, cardamom pods, cumin and coriander seeds, 2 tablespoons of the lemon juice, nutmeg, bay leaves and oil in a food processor or blender and blend to a paste.

2 Put the steak in a bowl, add the paste and stir well. Cover loosely and leave to marinate for at least 4 hours or overnight. Meanwhile, soak 8 wooden skewers in water.

3 Put the peanut butter, sugar, chilli, soy sauce, stock and the remaining lemon juice in a small saucepan and heat gently until the mixture has thickened.

4 Thread the meat on to the skewers and arrange them on a foil-lined baking sheet or shallow tin. (You will need to cook the beef skewers in batches.) Place the beef on the upper rack of the halogen oven.

5 Set the temperature to 250°C (482°F) and cook 4 of the beef skewers for 5–8 minutes on each side, until golden brown. Transfer to a warm serving dish while you cook the remainder. Check the sauce for seasoning and serve with the beef, steamed rice and lime quarters.

prep + cook time 55 minutes + marinating time
serves 4–5

CHILLI-SPICED MEATBALLS

1 large onion, roughly chopped
1 fresh red chilli, deseeded and
   chopped
2 garlic cloves, chopped
1 teaspoon shrimp paste
2 teaspoons coriander seeds
2 teaspoons cumin seeds
450 g (14½ oz) lean minced beef
2 teaspoons dark soy sauce
1 teaspoon dark muscovado
   sugar
juice of ½ lemon
1 egg, beaten
vegetable oil, for oiling
salt and pepper
finely sliced spring onions,
   to garnish

to serve
noodles
sweet chilli dipping sauce

1 Put the onion, chilli, garlic and shrimp paste in a food processor and process to a paste, or grind to a paste using a mortar and pestle. (Don't overmix or the onion will become too wet.)

2 Heat the coriander and cumin seeds in a small frying pan on the hob until they start to release their aroma. Grind in a pestle and mortar. Put the minced beef in a mixing bowl and add the onion mixture, toasted coriander and cumin seeds, soy sauce, sugar and lemon juice. Add the beaten egg and mix until evenly combined. (This is best done with your hands.)

3 Shape the mixture into balls, each about the size of a golf ball. Lightly oil a shallow roasting tin or ovenproof dish and add the meatballs. Place on the upper rack of the halogen oven.

4 Set the temperature to 200°C (392°F) and grill the meatballs for 12–15 minutes, turning halfway through cooking, until cooked through. Serve with noodles and sweet chilli dipping sauce, garnished with finely sliced spring onions.

prep + cook time 40 minutes
serves 4

LAMB CHOPS WITH GINGER & ORANGE

4 large chump chops
2 tablespoons vegetable oil
1 large onion, finely chopped
1 whole orange, plus the finely
    grated rind of 1 orange and
    2 tablespoons juice
2 tablespoons sun-dried tomato
    paste
1 tablespoon light muscovado
    sugar
15 g (½ oz) fresh root ginger,
    grated
300 ml (½ pint) hot lamb or
    chicken stock
2 teaspoons cornflour
salt and pepper

to serve
basmati rice
watercress salad

1 Season the chops on both sides with salt and pepper. Heat 1 tablespoon of the oil in a frying pan on the hob and fry the chops until lightly browned on both sides. Transfer to a casserole dish.
2 Add the onion to the frying pan and fry gently for about 5 minutes until softened. Add to the dish.
3 Mix together the orange rind and juice, tomato paste, sugar, ginger and stock in a jug. Add a little seasoning and pour the mixture over the chops. Cover with foil and place on the lower rack of the halogen oven.
4 Set the temperature to 200°C (392°F) and cook for about 30 minutes or until the meat is tender. Remove the chops from the dish.
5 Blend the cornflour with 2 tablespoons water and stir into the casserole juices. Return the lamb to the dish and cook, uncovered, for a further 5–10 minutes or until the juices have thickened slightly.

6 Meanwhile, cut the whole orange in half widthways, then into quarters. Heat the remaining oil in the frying pan and lightly sear the orange pieces on the cut sides. Serve with the lamb, accompanied by basmati rice and a watercress salad.

prep + cook time about 1 hour
serves 4

LAMB HOTPOT

4 lean lamb chops
25 g (1 oz) butter
1 onion, thinly sliced
1 teaspoon chopped rosemary
1 garlic clove, crushed
2 medium potatoes, thinly sliced
200 ml (7 fl oz) hot lamb or
    chicken stock
salt and pepper
green vegetables, to serve

1 Trim any excess fat from the lamb and season lightly on both sides with salt and pepper.
2 Reserve a little piece of the butter and melt the remainder in a frying pan on the hob and fry the chops until lightly brown. Transfer to a shallow casserole dish. Add the onion, rosemary and garlic to the frying pan and fry for 3 minutes. Scatter on top of the lamb.
3 Layer the potatoes on top and pour over the stock. Dot with the reserved butter, season lightly and cover with foil. Place the dish on the lower rack of the halogen oven.
4 Set the temperature to 200°C (392°F) and cook for 30–40 minutes until the potatoes are tender. Remove the foil and cook for a further 5–8 minutes until the surface is golden. Serve with seasonal green vegetables.

prep + cook time about 1 hour 15 minutes
serves 2

LAMB TIKKA KEBABS WITH CUCUMBER SALAD

150 ml (¼ pint) natural yogurt
1 garlic clove, crushed
1 teaspoon ground coriander
juice of ½ lemon
1 tablespoon chopped parsley
½ teaspoon ground turmeric
1 teaspoon chilli powder
1 teaspoon garam masala
450 g (14½ oz) lamb tenderloin,
    cut into 2.5 cm (1 inch) pieces
coriander sprigs, to garnish

cucumber salad
1 cucumber
1 garlic clove, crushed
1 tablespoon chopped mint
1 teaspoon caster sugar
150 ml (¼ pint) natural yogurt

to serve
flat bread
lime quarters

1 In a large bowl mix together the yogurt, garlic, coriander, lemon juice, parsley, turmeric, chilli powder and garam masala. Add the lamb and stir to mix. Cover loosely and refrigerate for at least 4 hours or overnight. Meanwhile, soak 8 wooden skewers in cold water.
2 Thread the lamb on to the skewers and place them on the upper rack of the halogen oven.
3 Set the temperature to 225°C (437°F) and cook the kebabs for about 15 minutes, turning them a couple of times so they cook evenly.
4 Meanwhile, make the salad. Peel and halve the cucumber and discard the seeds. Dice the flesh and mix it in a bowl with the garlic, mint, sugar and yogurt.
5 Garnish the kebabs with coriander sprigs and serve with the salad, warm flat bread and lime quarters.

prep + cook time 35 minutes + marinating time
serves 4

SUMMER ROAST LAMB

2 tablespoons olive oil
3 tablespoons red wine
2 teaspoons ground cumin
2 teaspoons hot paprika
1 teaspoon coarsely ground
    black pepper
1.5 kg (3 lb) leg of lamb
2 garlic cloves, thinly sliced
salt

to serve
Greek salad
pitta bread

1 Mix together the oil, wine, cumin, paprika and black pepper in a small bowl.

2 Place the lamb in a shallow dish and make small slits over the surface. Push a slice of garlic into each slit. Spoon over the spice mixture and spread it all over the lamb. Cover loosely with clingfilm and leave to marinate in the refrigerator for several hours, occasionally spooning the marinade over the meat. Place the lamb on the lower rack of the halogen oven.

3 Set the temperature to 250°C (482°F) and roast the lamb for 15 minutes. Reduce the temperature to 200°C (392°F) and roast for a further 25–30 minutes, spreading with the leftover marinade in the dish during cooking. (The lamb will be slightly pink in the centre; cook for a little longer if you prefer it well done.)

4 Transfer to a carving platter or board, and leave to rest for 20 minutes before carving. Serve with a Greek salad and warm pitta bread.

prep + cook time 1 hour + marinating & resting time
serves 6

ROAST STUFFED SHOULDER OF LAMB

2 garlic cloves, crushed
2 tablespoons olive oil
1.5 kg (3 lb) boned shoulder
   of lamb
100 g (3½ oz) bread, sliced
50 g (2 oz) butter
1 onion, chopped
4 celery sticks, chopped
4 tablespoons chopped parsley
½ teaspoon cayenne pepper
200 ml (7 fl oz) red wine
2 tablespoons clear honey
salt and pepper

1 Mix together the garlic and oil with a little salt and pepper. Brush over the lamb. Cover and chill.
2 Arrange the slices of bread in a single layer on the baking sheet and place on the upper rack of the halogen oven. Set the temperature to 250°C (482°F) and cook for about 5 minutes until toasted, watching closely so that the bread does not brown too much. Cut into small dice.
3 Melt the butter in a frying pan on the hob and fry the onion and celery for 5 minutes to soften. Tip into a bowl and stir in the toasted bread, parsley, cayenne and a little salt. Lay the lamb on a board, skin-side down, and pack the stuffing into the cavity. Secure the ends with skewers to hold the stuffing in place. Place the lamb on the lower rack of the halogen oven and cover with foil.

4 Set the temperature to 200°C (392°F) and cook for 45 minutes. Remove the foil and cook for 15 minutes to brown the meat. Transfer the meat to a board or platter and leave to rest for 20 minutes before carving.
5 Meanwhile, skim off the fat from the bowl of the oven and add the red wine and honey. Season with salt and pepper. Cook for 5 minutes until the gravy is hot. Transfer to a jug and serve with the lamb.

prep + cook time 1 hour 25 minutes + resting time
serves 6

EASY LAMB CURRY

25 g (1 oz) butter
2 tablespoons vegetable oil
350 g (11½ oz) lean lamb, diced
1 onion, sliced
2 garlic cloves, chopped
1 cinnamon stick, halved
6 cardamom pods, crushed to
  open
1 teaspoon each of ground
  cumin, ginger and chilli powder
2 teaspoons garam masala
salt
chopped coriander, to garnish
basmati rice, to serve

1 Melt the butter with the oil in a frying pan on the hob and fry the lamb until browned. Transfer to a casserole dish.

2 Add the onion to the pan and fry gently for 5 minutes. Stir in the garlic and spices and fry for a further 2 minutes. Stir in 250 ml (8 fl oz) water and bring just to the boil. Pour over the lamb. Place on the lower rack of the halogen oven.

3 Set the temperature to 200°C (392°F) and cook for 20 minutes until the lamb is tender, stirring twice. Garnish with chopped coriander and serve with some basmati rice.

prep + cook time 40 minutes
serves 2

LOIN OF PORK WITH RED CABBAGE

450 g (14½ oz) red cabbage, thinly shredded
1 kg (2 lb) boned pork loin, skin scored
1 teaspoon celery salt
25 g (1 oz) butter
2 small onions, thinly sliced
2 dessert apples, peeled, cored and sliced
2 tablespoons red wine vinegar
2 tablespoons dark muscovado sugar
4 whole star anise
salt and pepper
mashed potatoes, to serve

1 Bring a saucepan of water to the boil. Add the cabbage and cook for 1 minute. Drain and rinse under cold running water.

2 Remove the skin from the pork and rub it with a little salt. Season the pork with celery salt and pepper. Melt the butter in a frying pan on the hob and fry the pork on all sides to brown. Remove from the pan.

3 Add the onions to the pan and fry gently for 5 minutes. Stir in the apples, vinegar, sugar, star anise and cabbage and mix well. Turn the mixture into a large ovenproof dish and rest the pork on top, nestling it down into the cabbage. Cover with foil and place on the lower rack of the halogen oven.

4 Set the temperature to 200°C (392°F) and cook for 30 minutes. Remove and discard the foil. Remove the crackling and set aside. Return the meat to the oven and cook for a further 30 minutes until it is cooked through. Transfer the meat to a board or platter, cover with foil and leave to rest for 20 minutes before carving.

5 While the pork is resting, put the crackling skin-side up on the lower rack of the halogen oven. Set the temperature to 225°C (437°F) and cook for 20–25 minutes until crispy and golden. Separate the crackling into pieces and serve with the pork, cabbage and buttery mashed potatoes.

prep + cook time 1 hour 50 minutes + resting time
serves 4

POT ROASTED PORK WITH APPLES & CIDER

1.5 kg (3 lb) boned and rolled leg
of pork
4 tablespoons vegetable oil
several rosemary sprigs
1.25 kg (2½ lb) potatoes, thickly
sliced
2 dessert apples, cored and
thickly sliced
1 onion, sliced
175 ml (6 fl oz) dry cider
salt and pepper
seasonal vegetables, to serve

1 If not already scored, use a
sharp knife to score the skin of
the pork at 1 cm (½ inch) intervals.
Sprinkle with salt and drizzle with
1 tablespoon of the oil. Rub over
the surface of the skin. Scatter the
rosemary into a roasting tin, place
the pork on top and put it on the
lower rack of the halogen oven.
2 Set the temperature to 200°C
(392°F) and cook for 45 minutes.
3 Meanwhile, cook the potatoes
in a large saucepan of boiling,
lightly salted water for 5 minutes
until beginning to soften. Drain
thoroughly and toss with the
remaining oil.
4 Scatter the apples and onion
around the pork and pour over the
cider. Arrange the potatoes on top
and season to taste with salt and
pepper.
5 Return to the oven and cook for
a further 20–25 minutes until the
pork is cooked through and the
potatoes are golden. Leave to rest
for 20 minutes before serving with
seasonal vegetables.

prep + cook time 1 hour
30 minutes + resting time
serves 6

PESTO PORK WITH TOMATOES

2 tablespoons olive oil
1 small onion, finely chopped
4 tablespoons sun-dried tomato
  pesto
1 teaspoon dried oregano
25 g (1 oz) breadcrumbs
4 pieces of pork tenderloin, each
  150 g (5 oz)
15 g (½ oz) butter
2 teaspoons plain flour
300 ml (½ pint) dry white wine
8 pitted green olives, roughly
  sliced
100 g (3½ oz) cherry tomatoes,
  halved
finely grated rind of 1 lemon
2 tablespoons chopped parsley
salt and pepper
pasta, to serve

1 Heat 1 tablespoon of the oil in a small frying pan on the hob and gently fry the onion for 5 minutes. Remove from the heat and stir in the pesto, oregano, breadcrumbs and a little seasoning. Leave to cool.

2 Make a horizontal cut through each piece of pork so that the meat is almost sliced in half. Open out the pieces and place them between sheets of baking parchment. Beat them with a rolling pin or meat mallet to flatten slightly.

3 Spread the tomato mixture evenly over the pork and fold the pieces back in half. Secure with string at 3 cm (1¼ inch) intervals. Heat the remaining oil in the frying pan and lightly brown the pork on all sides. Transfer to a shallow ovenproof dish.

4 Melt the butter in the frying pan, add the flour and stir over a gentle heat for 30 seconds. Gradually blend in the wine and bring to the boil. Pour the mixture over the pork, cover the dish with foil and place on the lower rack of the halogen oven.

5 Set the temperature to 200°C (392°F) and cook for 25 minutes. Add the olives and cherry tomatoes to the dish and cook, uncovered, for a further 5 minutes or until the meat is cooked through. Check the seasoning and sprinkle with chopped parsley. Serve with fresh ribbon pasta.

prep + cook time about 1 hour
serves 4

PORK CHOPS ARDENNAISE

4 pork loin chops, 200 g
  (7 oz) each
25 g (1 oz) butter
1 tablespoon vegetable oil
100 g (3½ oz) button mushrooms,
  halved
100 g (3½ oz) diced pancetta
12 shallots, peeled and left whole
300 ml (½ pint) dry white wine
1 tablespoon cornflour
2 tablespoons water
1 tablespoon French mustard
150 ml (¼ pint) single cream
salt and pepper
chopped parsley, to garnish

1 Season the pork chops with salt and pepper. Melt the butter with the oil in a frying pan on the hob and fry the chops on both sides to brown. Transfer to a casserole dish. Add the mushrooms, pancetta and shallots to the same frying pan and fry gently, stirring, for 5 minutes. Add to the casserole.

2 Pour the wine into the pan and bring to the boil, letting it bubble for a minute and scraping up any bits from the bottom of the pan. Tip into the casserole and cover with foil. Place on the lower rack of the halogen oven.

3 Set the temperature to 200°C (392°F) and cook for 30 minutes. In a small bowl, blend the cornflour with the measurement water. Remove the chops from the casserole and add the cornflour paste, mustard and cream to the liquid. Season to taste with salt and pepper, and return the pork to the dish. Cover and cook for a further 5 minutes. Serve hot, sprinkled with parsley.

prep + cook time about 1 hour
serves 4

CHICKEN & SEAFOOD

CHICKEN IN RED WINE

50 g (2 oz) butter
2 tablespoons olive oil
4 chicken drumsticks
4 chicken thighs
100 g (3½ oz) small shallots, peeled and left whole
50 g (2 oz) smoked streaky bacon, diced
2 carrots, diced
1 celery stick, diced
1 tablespoon plain flour
150 ml (¼ pint) chicken stock
300 ml (½ pint) red wine
3 tablespoons sun-dried tomato paste
3 garlic cloves, crushed
3 bay leaves
2 thick slices of white bread
salt and pepper
chopped parsley, to garnish

to serve
mashed potatoes
minted peas

1 Melt half the butter and oil in a frying pan on the hob and lightly brown the chicken on all sides. Transfer the chicken to a casserole dish.
2 Add the shallots, bacon, carrots and celery to the frying pan and cook gently for 6–8 minutes until beginning to brown. Sprinkle in the flour, stirring to mix. Gradually blend in the stock, wine and tomato paste. Add the garlic, bay leaves and a little seasoning. Bring to the boil and pour the mixture over the chicken. Cover with foil and place on the lower rack of the halogen oven.
3 Set the temperature to 200°C (392°F) and cook for 40–45 minutes or until the chicken is cooked through.
4 Meanwhile, remove the crusts from the bread and cut the rest of the bread into small cubes. Heat the remaining butter and oil in the cleaned frying pan and fry the bread, stirring, until lightly browned.

5 Remove the chicken from the oven and check the seasoning of the sauce. Serve with a scattering of croutons, creamy mashed potatoes and minted peas.

prep + cook time 1 hour 15 minutes
serves 4

SPANISH STUFFED CHICKEN WITH COUSCOUS

325 g (11 oz) can or jar pimientos
3 tablespoons olive oil
1 small onion, finely chopped
25 g (1 oz) blanched almonds,
    finely chopped
8 pitted green olives, chopped
1 large tomato, skinned,
    deseeded and chopped
50 g (2 oz) breadcrumbs
1.5 kg (3 lb) oven-ready chicken
salt and pepper
couscous, to serve

1   Thoroughly drain the pimientos, pat them dry on kitchen paper and cut them into small pieces.

2   Melt 2 tablespoons of the oil in a frying pan on the hob and gently fry the onion for 5 minutes to soften. Remove from the heat and stir in the pimientos, almonds, olives, tomato, breadcrumbs and a little seasoning.

3   Put the chicken on a board and remove the wishbone. Pack the stuffing into the neck cavity, wrap the skin under the bird and secure with a metal skewer. Shape the remaining stuffing into small balls.

4   Place the chicken on the lower rack of the halogen oven and brush with the remaining oil. Season with salt and pepper and place the stuffing balls around the chicken.

5   Set the temperature to 200°C (392°F) and cook for 40 minutes. Turn the chicken and meatballs and cook for a further 20–30 minutes. Cover the chicken and meatballs with foil if they are browning too fast. Check that the meat is cooked through by piercing the thickest area of the thigh with a knife or skewer; the juices should run clear. If necessary, cook the chicken for a little longer.

6   Leave the chicken to rest in a warm place for 15 minutes before carving. Serve with couscous.

prep + cook time 1 hour 25 minutes + resting time
serves 4–6

FIVE-SPICE CHICKEN

4 medium boneless, skinless
  chicken breasts, about 200 g
  (7 oz) each, cut into 2.5 cm
  (1 inch) chunks
2 shallots, thinly sliced
1 whole garlic clove
2 tablespoons light soy sauce
1 tablespoon dry sherry
½ teaspoon five-spice powder

to garnish
1 spring onion, finely chopped
sesame seeds
chopped coriander
steamed rice, to serve

1 Mix the chicken in a bowl with the shallots, garlic, soy sauce, sherry and five-spice powder. Cover loosely and leave to marinate in the refrigerator for at least 1 hour or overnight. Remove garlic from marinade and discard.

2 Place a sheet of foil over the upper rack of the halogen oven, turning the edges up so that the juices will be contained as the chicken cooks. Tip in the chicken and its marinade and spread in an even layer.

3 Set the temperature to 200°C (392°F) and cook for about 20 minutes, turning the chicken pieces occasionally so that they cook evenly. Serve sprinkled with the spring onion, sesame seeds and coriander, and accompany with steamed rice.

prep + cook time 30 minutes + marinating time
serves 4

MARINATED CHICKEN WITH SPICED YOGURT

1.5 kg (3 lb) oven-ready chicken, skin removed
450 ml (¾ pint) natural yogurt
2 garlic cloves, crushed
5 cm (2 inch) piece of fresh root ginger, finely chopped
2 dried chillies, crushed
½ teaspoon ground turmeric
1 teaspoon salt
½ teaspoon ground mixed spice
2 tablespoons chopped mint
1 tablespoon ground cumin
2 teaspoons caster sugar
pepper

to serve
basmati rice
herb salad

1 Put the chicken in a large bowl. In a separate bowl mix together 300 ml (½ pint) of the yogurt and the garlic, ginger, chillies, turmeric, salt, mixed spice, mint, cumin and sugar. Tip the mixture over the chicken, making sure the whole chicken is coated in marinade. Cover loosely and chill for at least 8 hours or overnight.
2 Transfer the chicken to a roasting tin and tip over any of the yogurt mixture left in the bowl. Place on the lower rack of the halogen oven.
3 Set the temperature to 200°C (392°F) and cook for 20 minutes. Turn the chicken and cook for a further 20 minutes. Cover the chicken with foil if it is browning too fast. Check that the meat is cooked through by piercing the thickest area of the thigh with a knife or skewer; the juices should run clear. If necessary cook for a little longer. Leave the chicken to rest in a warm place while you finish the sauce.

4 Pour the juices from the roasting tin into a serving jug and stir in the remaining yogurt. Check the seasoning and serve with the chicken, basmati rice and a herb salad.

prep + cook time 1 hour + marinating time
serves 4

STICKY GLAZED CHICKEN DRUMSTICKS

4 tablespoons red wine vinegar
2 tablespoons dark soy sauce
2 tablespoons tomato purée
2 garlic cloves, crushed
generous pinch of cayenne
    pepper
1 tablespoon Worcestershire
    sauce
2 tablespoons clear honey
8 large chicken drumsticks,
    skinned
vegetable oil for brushing

to serve
buttered corn on the cob
watercress salad

1 Mix together the vinegar, soy sauce, tomato purée, garlic, cayenne pepper, Worcestershire sauce and honey in a small bowl.
2 Make 2 or 3 deep slits in the fleshy side of each drumstick. Place in a shallow glass or ceramic dish and add the marinade, turning the chicken drumsticks until coated. Cover loosely with clingfilm and leave to marinate in the refrigerator for at least 2 hours, or overnight.
3 Place a sheet of foil over the upper rack of the halogen oven, turning up the edges so that the juices will be contained as the chicken cooks. Brush lightly with oil. Arrange the chicken on the foil and spoon over the marinade.
4 Set the temperature to 200°C (392°F) and cook for 25 minutes, turning the chicken occasionally and brushing with the marinade, until cooked through. Serve with buttered corn on the cob and a watercress salad.

prep + cook time 35 minutes
+ marinating time
serves 4

CHICKEN & MUSHROOM CASSEROLE

2 teaspoons plain flour
8 large boneless, skinless chicken
thighs, halved
25 g (1 oz) butter
1 onion, chopped
300 ml (½ pint) chicken stock
several rosemary sprigs
200 g (7 oz) chestnut mushrooms,
sliced
4 tablespoons crème fraîche
salt and pepper

to serve
celeriac and potato mash
seasonal vegetables

1 Season the flour with salt and pepper. Toss the chicken pieces in the flour.
2 Melt the butter in a frying pan on the hob and fry the chicken pieces and onion for 5 minutes or until beginning to brown. Pour in the stock, stir through and bring to the boil. Transfer to a casserole dish and add the rosemary, mushrooms and a little salt and pepper. Cover with foil and place on the lower rack of the halogen oven.
3 Set the temperature to 200°C (392°F) and cook for 30 minutes, removing the foil for the last 5 minutes of cooking time. Remove from the oven and stir in the crème fraîche. Check the seasoning and serve with celeriac and potato mash and seasonal vegetables.

prep + cook time 50 minutes
serves 4

COD FILLET WITH CORIANDER CREAM SAUCE

2 teaspoons plain flour
2 teaspoons ground coriander
4 cod fillets, each 200 g (7 oz)
2 tablespoons olive oil
1 tablespoon lemon juice
1 tablespoon capers
1 egg yolk
100 ml (3½ fl oz) single cream
salt and pepper
chopped coriander, to garnish

to serve
new potatoes
green salad

1 Mix the flour with the ground coriander and a little seasoning on a plate. Use the mixture to coat the cod fillets.

2 Put the oil in a shallow ovenproof dish and place it on the upper rack of the halogen oven. Set the temperature to 250°C (482°F) and heat the oil for 3 minutes. Add the fish portions and cook for 3–4 minutes on each side until just cooked through. (Test by piercing the fish with the tip of a knife; it should flake easily.) Drizzle with the lemon juice and scatter over the capers. Cook for a further 2 minutes.

3 Remove the fish to warm serving plates. Mix together the egg yolk and cream and stir into the juices remaining in the dish. Heat through for 3–4 minutes, season to taste and spoon over the fish. Serve garnished with chopped coriander and accompanied with new potatoes and a green salad.

prep + cook time 20 minutes
serves 4

HALIBUT WITH TOMATOES & BASIL

2 tablespoons lemon juice
5 tablespoons olive oil
4 halibut steaks
3 shallots, sliced
1 head of fennel, thinly sliced
300 g (10 oz) tomatoes, skinned,
   deseeded and chopped
3 tablespoons sun-dried tomato
   paste
2 teaspoons caster sugar
300 ml (½ pint) dry white wine
1 teaspoon fennel seeds, crushed
handful of basil leaves, shredded
salt and pepper
basil leaves, to garnish

to serve
crusty bread
green salad (optional)

1 Mix together the lemon juice, 3 tablespoons of the oil and a little salt and pepper. Spoon the mixture over the halibut and leave to marinate for 1–2 hours.

2 Heat the remaining oil in a large frying pan on the hob and gently fry the shallots and fennel for about 10 minutes until they are soft but not browned. Stir in the tomatoes, tomato paste, sugar, wine, fennel seeds, basil and seasoning and bring to the boil. Turn the mixture into a shallow ovenproof dish and place the halibut on top. Cover with foil and place on the lower rack of the halogen oven.

3 Set the temperature to 225°C (437°F) and cook for 20–25 minutes until the fish is cooked through. (Test by piercing with the tip of a knife; it should flake easily.) Check the seasoning and transfer to shallow bowls. Scatter with basil leaves and serve with warm crusty bread and a leafy green salad, if liked.

prep + cook time 55 minutes + marinating time
serves 4

MALAYSIAN PRAWN CURRY

2 tablespoons vegetable oil
2 onions, sliced
3 cm (1¼ inch) piece of fresh root ginger, finely chopped
2 garlic cloves, crushed
2 teaspoons cumin seeds, crushed
2 teaspoons coriander seeds, crushed
1 teaspoon dried chilli flakes
1 cinnamon stick
500 ml (17 fl oz) fish stock
2 tablespoons lime juice
1 tablespoon caster sugar
2 tablespoons light soy sauce
1 green pepper, cored, deseeded and diced
4 teaspoons cornflour
225 g (7½ oz) can pineapple slices in natural juice, drained (reserve the juice)
400 g (13 oz) raw peeled and deveined prawns
salt
noodles or rice, to serve

1 Heat the oil in a large frying pan or wok on the hob and fry the onions for about 8 minutes until they begin to brown. Stir in the ginger, garlic, cumin and coriander seeds, chilli flakes and cinnamon and cook for a further 2 minutes.

2 Pour in the stock and add the lime juice, sugar, soy sauce and green pepper and bring almost to the boil. Pour the mixture into an ovenproof casserole dish and cover with foil. Place on the lower rack of the halogen oven.

3 Set the temperature to 225°C (437°F) and cook for 15 minutes.

4 Meanwhile, blend the cornflour with 4 tablespoons of the reserved pineapple juice in a small bowl. Chop the pineapple pieces and add them to the casserole along with the cornflour paste and the prawns. Cook, uncovered, for a further 10 minutes or until the sauce has thickened and the prawns are pink and cooked through. Serve with sesame noodles or steamed rice.

prep + cook time about 1 hour
serves 4

FAMILY FISH PIE

1 kg (2 lb) floury potatoes
625 g (1¼ lb) cod, pollack or
   haddock fillet, skinned
600 ml (1 pint) milk
100 g (3½ oz) butter
1 onion, finely chopped
2 celery sticks, thinly sliced
2 tablespoons chopped parsley
40 g (1½ oz) plain flour
100 g (3½ oz) mature Cheddar
   cheese, grated
100 ml (3½ fl oz) single cream
   or milk
salt and pepper

1 Cook the potatoes in a large saucepan of boiling, lightly salted water for 20 minutes or until tender. Drain and return to the pan. Set aside.

2 Meanwhile, put the fish in a shallow ovenproof dish with half the milk and place on the lower rack of the halogen oven.

3 Set the temperature to 225°C (437°F) and cook for 15 minutes until the fish is cooked through. Pour off the milk, reserving it for the sauce, and flake the fish evenly over the bottom of the dish.

4 Melt 25 g (1 oz) of the butter in a saucepan and gently fry the onion and celery for about 5 minutes until softened. Spoon the onion–celery mixture over the flaked fish and scatter over the parsley.

5 Make the sauce. Melt a further 50 g (2 oz) of the butter in a clean saucepan and stir in the flour to make a smooth paste. Remove from the heat and gradually blend in all the reserved milk. Return to the heat and bring to the boil, stirring continuously, until thickened. Stir in half the cheese and season to taste with salt and pepper. Spoon over the fish.

6 Mash the potatoes with the cream and remaining butter and season to taste. Add the potatoes to the dish, spreading them in an even layer over the fish. Scatter the remaining cheese over the potatoes, cover the pie with foil and place on the lower rack of the halogen oven.

7 Set the temperature to 200°C (392°F) and cook for 25 minutes. Remove the foil and cook for a further 10–15 minutes until the surface is golden.

prep + cook time 1½ hours
serves 4

SPICY CRAB CAKES

1 tablespoon vegetable oil, plus a
  little extra for drizzling
½ bunch of spring onions, thinly
  sliced, plus extra, cut into strips
  and dropped into cold water to
  make curls, to garnish
2 garlic cloves, crushed
1 fresh red chilli, deseeded and
  finely chopped
350 g (11½ oz) crabmeat
2 teaspoons tomato ketchup
4 tablespoons mayonnaise
2 teaspoons Worcestershire sauce
175 g (6 oz) dried breadcrumbs
50 g (2 oz) plain flour
1 egg
salt and pepper
sweet chilli sauce or mayonnaise,
  to serve

1 Heat the oil in a frying pan on the hob and gently fry the sliced spring onions for 2 minutes. Stir in the garlic and chilli, then tip the contents of the pan into a bowl. Leave to cool.

2 Add the crabmeat, ketchup, mayonnaise, Worcestershire sauce and 50 g (2 oz) of the breadcrumbs to the bowl, season with a little salt and pepper and stir well to mix. Shape the mixture into 12 cakes.

3 Season the flour with salt and pepper on a plate. Beat the egg on a second plate and scatter the remaining breadcrumbs on a third. Dust the fishcakes with the flour, then coat in the egg and breadcrumbs.

4 Drizzle a little extra oil into a shallow roasting tin and space the fishcakes slightly apart in the tin. (You may need to cook them in 2 batches.) Drizzle with more oil and place on the upper rack of the halogen oven.

5 Set the temperature to 200°C (392°F) and cook the fishcakes for 8–10 minutes, turning over halfway through cooking. Serve with extra mayonnaise or sweet chilli sauce, scattered with spring onion curls.

prep + cook time about
40 minutes + cooling time
serves 6

VEGETARIAN

LEEK & CHESTNUT PARCELS

75 g (3 oz) butter
2 small leeks, trimmed and
    chopped
75 g (3 oz) cooked chestnuts,
    chopped
4 tablespoons single cream
2 tablespoons chopped parsley
freshly grated nutmeg
300 g (10 oz) filo pastry, cut into
    24 x 12 cm (5 inch) squares
salt and pepper

dressing
4 tablespoons extra virgin olive
    oil
1 tablespoon white wine vinegar
1 teaspoon clear honey
1 teaspoon wholegrain mustard
rocket, to serve

1 Melt 25 g (1 oz) of the butter in a frying pan on the hob and gently fry the leeks until very soft. Leave to cool. Add the chopped chestnuts, cream, parsley and plenty of nutmeg. Season lightly with salt and pepper. Melt the remaining butter in a small saucepan.

2 Brush 4 of the filo squares lightly with melted butter and position a second square on top, adjusting the angle to create a star shape. Brush lightly with more butter and position a third layer, again adjusting the angle. Divide half the filling equally among the centres. Lift up the pastry edges and pinch together to parcels.

3 Repeat with the remainder of the pastry and filling, so that you end up with 8 parcels, and place in a shallow roasting tin. Brush with the remaining butter. Place on the lower rack of the halogen oven.

4 Set the temperature to 200°C (392°F) and cook for 10–15 minutes until the pastry is golden and crisp. While cooking, mix together the dressing ingredients in a small bowl. Arrange the filo parcels on a bed of rocket and drizzle with the dressing.

prep + cook time 40 minutes
serves 8

CHICKPEA & PEPPER CHILLI

3 tablespoons olive oil
1 large onion, chopped
2 celery sticks, chopped
2 courgettes, chopped
2 red peppers, cored, deseeded and chopped
3 garlic cloves, crushed
2 teaspoons dried oregano
2 teaspoons cumin seeds, lightly crushed
400 g (13 oz) can chickpeas, rinsed and drained
800 g (1 lb 10 oz) can plum tomatoes
2 tablespoons black treacle
1 tablespoon wine vinegar
salt and pepper

to serve
rice
soured cream
chopped coriander

1 Heat the oil in a frying pan on the hob and add the onion and celery. Fry gently for 5 minutes, then add the courgettes, peppers, garlic, oregano and cumin. Fry gently for a further 5 minutes. Turn into a casserole dish and stir in the chickpeas.

2 Tip the tomatoes into the frying pan and add the treacle and vinegar. Bring to the boil and add to the casserole dish, stirring the ingredients to combine. Cover the casserole dish with foil and place on the lower rack of the halogen oven.

3 Set the temperature to 175°C (347°F) and cook for 50 minutes until thick and pulpy. Check the seasoning and serve in bowls over a bed of steamed rice. Top with spoonfuls of soured cream and scatter with chopped coriander leaves.

prep + cook time 1 hour 20 minutes
serves 4

VEGETABLE STEW WITH HERB DUMPLINGS

25 g (1 oz) butter
1 onion, chopped
1 leek, thickly sliced
3 carrots, roughly chopped
2 celery sticks, roughly chopped
2 garlic cloves, crushed
2 tablespoons plain flour
1 litre (1¾ pints) vegetable stock
4 tablespoons sun-dried tomato pesto
400 g (13 oz) can haricot beans, rinsed and drained
150 g (5 oz) self-raising flour
75 g (3 oz) vegetable suet
25 g (1 oz) Parmesan cheese, grated
1 tablespoon chopped oregano, to garnish
salt and pepper

1 Melt the butter in a large saucepan on the hob and gently fry the onion for about 5 minutes until softened. Stir in the leek, carrots, celery and garlic and cook, stirring frequently, for a further 5 minutes.

2 Add the plain flour and cook for 1 minute. Gradually blend in the stock and cook, stirring, for 5 minutes or until slightly thickened. Stir in the pesto and beans. Turn the mixture into a casserole dish, cover with greased foil and place on the lower rack of the halogen oven.

3 Set the temperature to 225°C (437°F) and cook for about 30 minutes until the vegetables are almost tender.

4 Meanwhile, in a bowl mix together the self-raising flour, suet, Parmesan and oregano. Season to taste with salt and pepper. Add about 125 ml (4 fl oz) water and mix with a round-bladed knife to form a soft dough, adding a little more water if the dough feels dry.

5 Place dessertspoonfuls of the dumpling mixture over the stew and loosely re-cover dish with foil. Cook for a further 20 minutes or until the dumplings are light and fluffy. Serve garnished with chopped oregano.

prep + cook time 1 hour 20 minutes
serves 4

WARM ASPARAGUS & HALOUMI SALAD

5 tablespoons extra virgin
  olive oil
1 tablespoon lemon juice
1 teaspoon caster sugar
1 tablespoon finely chopped
  parsley
400 g (13 oz) haloumi cheese,
  cut into thin slices
375 g (12 oz) fresh asparagus
2 tablespoons capers, rinsed and
  drained
salt and pepper

to serve
lemon wedges
grainy bread

1 Mix together 4 tablespoons of the oil, the lemon juice, sugar and parsley in a small bowl. Season with salt and pepper. Set aside.
2 Pat the cheese slices dry on kitchen paper. Brush the asparagus with the remaining oil and a little seasoning. Place the asparagus on the upper rack of the halogen oven.
3 Set the temperature to 200°C (392°F) and cook for 5 minutes. Transfer to the lower rack to keep warm. Place the haloumi slices on the upper rack and cook for a couple of minutes on each side. (You will need to cook the cheese in batches.)
4 Arrange the asparagus and haloumi on serving plates and scatter with the capers. Lightly whisk the dressing and drizzle over the salad. Serve with lemon wedges and grainy bread.

prep + cook time about 30 minutes
serves 6

STILTON & LEEK GRATIN

100 g (3½ oz) butter
3 large leeks, trimmed and sliced
100 g (3½ oz) plain flour
25 g (1 oz) Parmesan or pecorino
  cheese, grated
150 g (5 oz) Stilton cheese,
  crumbled
1 tablespoon capers
150 ml (¼ pint) single cream
salt and pepper
spinach and watercress salad,
  to serve

1 Put 25 g (1 oz) of the butter in a shallow ovenproof dish and place it on the lower rack of the halogen oven.

2 Set the temperature to 200°C (392°F) and heat for 3 minutes until the butter has melted. Add the leeks, turning them in the melted butter, and cook for a further 10 minutes, stirring frequently until softened.

3 Meanwhile, put the flour in a food processor or blender with the remaining butter and blend until the mixture resembles breadcrumbs. Add the Parmesan or pecorino, a little salt and plenty of pepper and blend lightly to mix.

4 Scatter the Stilton and capers over the leeks and drizzle with the cream. Sprinkle the crumble mixture over the top and pat down lightly. Reduce the temperature to 175°C (347°F) and cook for 15 minutes. Then increase the temperature to 200°C (392°F) and cook for a further 5–10 minutes until the topping is golden and the leeks are tender. Serve with a spinach and watercress salad.

prep + cook time 55 minutes
serves 3–4

GORGONZOLA & ROCKET PIZZA

250 g (8 oz) strong white flour, plus extra for dusting
2½ teaspoons fast-action dried yeast
1 teaspoon salt
3 tablespoons olive oil

topping
2 tablespoons olive oil
1 onion, chopped
2 garlic cloves, crushed
400 g (13 oz) can chopped tomatoes
2 tablespoons sun-dried tomato paste
2 tablespoons pesto
1 teaspoon mixed dried herbs
250 g (8 oz) Gorgonzola cheese
salt and pepper

to serve
rocket leaves
balsamic vinegar

1 Make the dough. In a bowl mix together the flour, yeast, salt and oil and add 125 ml (4 fl oz) hand-hot water. Mix with a round-bladed knife to make a dough, adding a dash more water if the mixture feels dry.
2 Turn out the dough on to a lightly floured surface and knead for about 10 minutes until smooth and elastic. Place in a lightly oiled bowl, cover with clingfilm and leave to rise in a warm place for about 1 hour or until doubled in size.
3 Prepare the topping. Heat the oil in a frying pan on the hob and gently fry the onion for 5 minutes. Stir in the garlic, tomatoes, tomato paste, pesto and herbs. Season to taste with salt and pepper and cook for about 15 minutes until thickened.

4 Lightly oil a pizza tray. Tip the dough out on to a lightly floured surface and roll out to a round slightly smaller than the tray. Transfer to the tray and spread the tomato topping over the surface. Crumble the Gorgonzola over the topping. Place on the upper rack of the halogen oven.
5 Set the temperature to 175°C (347°F) and cook for 25–30 minutes. Serve scattered with rocket leaves and drizzled with balsamic vinegar.

prep + cook time 1 hour 15 minutes + proving
serves 4

ON THE SIDE

SPICY SWEET POTATOES

10 cardamom pods
2 large sweet potatoes
3 tablespoons garlic- and
  herb-infused olive oil
½ teaspoon coriander seeds,
  crushed
½ teaspoon cumin seeds, crushed
salt and pepper
spicy or soured cream and herb
  dip, to serve

1 Use a pestle and mortar to crush the cardamom pods and release the seeds. Remove the shells and crush the seeds a little more.

2 Scrub the sweet potatoes and cut them into thick slices. Cook in a large saucepan of boiling, lightly salted water for 3 minutes until softened but not falling apart. Drain well.

3 Mix together the oil, coriander, cardamom and cumin seeds and a little salt and pepper. Drizzle the mixture over the potatoes, turning the slices until they are evenly coated. Arrange the potatoes in a single layer on the upper rack of the halogen oven. (You will need to cook the potatoes in batches.)

4 Set the temperature to 250°C (482°F) and cook for 5–8 minutes on each side until golden. Keep the potatoes warm while you cook the remainder. Serve as a snack with a spicy or soured cream and herb dip or to accompany roast pork or chicken.

prep + cook time about 35 minutes
serves 4

CARAMEL ROASTED VEGETABLES

1 small butternut squash
2 small sweet potatoes
1 aubergine
2 parsnips
2 carrots
2 tablespoons olive oil
4 cm (1¾ inch) piece of fresh root
  ginger, sliced
40 g (1½ oz) dark muscovado
  sugar
3 tablespoons dark soy sauce
juice of 1 lime
2 small red onions, thinly sliced
2 garlic cloves, thinly sliced

1 Scoop out the seeds and cut away the skin from the squash. Scrub the sweet potatoes. Cut the squash, potatoes and aubergine into 2.5 cm (1 inch) cubes. Cut the parsnips and carrots into wedges.
2 Mix together the oil, ginger, sugar, soy sauce and lime juice. Add the squash, potatoes, aubergine, parsnips, carrots and onions, turning the vegetables in the dressing until they are evenly coated. Scatter into a shallow roasting tin or ovenproof dish, cover with foil and place on the lower rack of the halogen oven.
3 Set the temperature to 200°C (392°F) and cook for 20 minutes. Remove the foil, add the garlic and stir well. Cook, uncovered, stirring occasionally, for a further 10–15 minutes or until caramelized. Serve with roast or grilled chicken, pork or duck.

prep + cook time 50 minutes
serves 4

ROOT VEGETABLE GRATIN

125 g (4 oz) butter
3 garlic cloves, crushed
2 tablespoons chopped thyme
plenty of freshly grated nutmeg
750 g (1½ lb) potatoes (such as
   Maris Piper)
450 g (14½ oz) carrots
400 g (13 oz) celeriac
300 g (10 oz) swede
100 ml (3½ fl oz) hot vegetable
   or chicken stock
salt and pepper

1 Melt the butter in a small saucepan on the hob and stir in the garlic, thyme and nutmeg. Season to taste with salt and pepper.

2 Slice the potatoes, carrots, celeriac and swede as thinly as possible. (A food processor with a slicer attachment or a mandolin slicer is ideal.) Layer the vegetables in an ovenproof dish, drizzling over a little of the flavoured butter as you assemble the dish.

3 Pour over the hot stock, cover the dish with foil and place on the lower rack of the halogen oven.

4 Set the temperature to 250°C (482°F) and cook for 1–1¼ hours or until the vegetables feel tender when pierced with a knife. Remove the foil and bake for a further 5–10 minutes or until the surface is golden. Serve with roast meats or poultry.

prep + cook time about 1¾ hours
serves 8

CHILLI PARSNIP CHIPS WITH SOURED CREAM

500 g (1 lb) small parsnips
3 tablespoons vegetable oil
½ teaspoon celery salt
1 teaspoon ground cumin
1 teaspoon ground coriander
4 tablespoons sweet chilli dipping
  sauce
chopped coriander leaves, to
  garnish (optional)
soured cream, to serve

1 Cut the parsnips lengthways into quarters and put them in a large bowl. Mix the oil with the celery salt, cumin and coriander and add to the bowl, turning the parsnips until they are evenly coated. Transfer the parsnips to a shallow roasting tin and place on the upper rack of the halogen oven.

2 Set the temperature to 250°C (482°F) and cook for about 20 minutes, turning the parsnips frequently until tender and turning golden. Brush with the chilli sauce and cook for a further 5 minutes.

3 Transfer to serving plates and scatter with the coriander, if using. Serve each portion with a pot of soured cream for dipping. Serve as a snack or with pork or lamb chops.

prep + cook time 35 minutes
serves 4

CORIANDER & GARLIC NAAN

650 g (1 lb 5 oz) strong white flour, plus extra for dusting
1 teaspoon salt
1 teaspoon caster sugar
2 teaspoons easy-blend dried yeast
75 g (3 oz) butter, plus extra for greasing
handful of chopped coriander
2 garlic cloves, crushed
275 ml (9 fl oz) warm milk
2 tablespoons natural yogurt

1 Put the flour, salt, sugar and yeast in a large bowl. Melt 50 g (2 oz) of the butter and stir in along with the coriander, garlic, warm milk and yogurt. Mix with a round-bladed knife to make a dough, adding a dash more milk if the dough is crumbly.

2 Turn the dough out on to a floured surface and knead for about 10 minutes until the dough is smooth and elastic. Place in a lightly oiled bowl, cover with clingfilm and leave to rise in a warm place for about 1 hour or until doubled in size.

3 Tip the dough out on to a lightly floured surface and cut into 8 even-sized pieces. Roll each into a ball, cover with a clean tea towel and leave to stand for 10 minutes. Thinly roll out each ball into a large teardrop shape and place on a floured tray.

4 Melt the remaining butter and brush a little over 2 of the breads. Transfer to a shallow greased baking sheet and place on the upper rack of the halogen oven.

5 Set the temperature to 250°C (482°F) and cook for about 6 minutes until puffed and golden. Stack on a plate and cover with a tea towel while you cook the remaining flat breads in the same way.

prep + cook time 50 minutes + proving
makes 8

SUN-DRIED TOMATO BREAD

75 g (3 oz) lightly salted butter, softened
6 sun-dried tomatoes in oil, finely drained and chopped
3 garlic cloves, crushed
finely grated rind of 1 lemon
3 tablespoons chopped parsley
1 large ciabatta loaf
salt and pepper

1 Beat together the butter, tomatoes, garlic, lemon rind and parsley with a little salt and pepper.

2 Make deep diagonal cuts, 2 cm (¾ inch) apart, down the length of the bread, keeping the bread intact underneath. Spread the flavoured butter into the cuts, spreading any excess butter over the top of the bread. Wrap in foil, with the opening along the top of the bread, and place on the lower rack of the halogen oven.

3 Set the temperature to 250°C (482°F) and cook for 8–10 minutes until the butter has melted into the bread. Open out the top of the foil and cook for a further 4–5 minutes until the surface is golden.

prep + cook time 35 minutes
serves 6

SWEET TREATS

CARDAMOM & SULTANA TEACAKES

12 cardamom pods

450 g (14½ oz) strong white bread flour, plus extra for dusting

75 g (3 oz) caster sugar

½ teaspoon salt

2 teaspoons fast-action dried yeast

300 ml (½ pint) warm milk, plus extra to glaze

50 g (2 oz) unsalted butter, melted

1 teaspoon vanilla bean paste or extract

125 g (4 oz) sultanas

1 Use a pestle and mortar to crush the cardamom pods to release the seeds. Remove the shells and crush the seeds a little more.

2 Put the seeds into a bowl and add the flour, sugar, salt and yeast. Mix the milk in jug with the butter and vanilla paste or extract and add to the dry ingredients. Mix with a round-bladed knife to form a soft dough, adding a little more milk if the dough is dry.

3 Turn the dough out on to a lightly floured surface and knead for about 10 minutes until smooth and elastic. Drop the dough into a lightly oiled bowl, cover with clingfilm and leave to rise in a warm place for about 1 hour or until doubled in size.

4 Tip the dough out on to a lightly floured surface and knead in the sultanas. Cover with a cloth and leave to stand for 10 minutes. Divide the dough into 9 equal pieces and roll each into a ball. Set them, spaced slightly apart, on a greased baking sheet and cover loosely with oiled clingfilm.

Leave to stand for about 40 minutes or until doubled in size. (The buns will be meeting at the edges but can be separated after cooking.) Brush with a little milk and place on the lower rack of the halogen oven.

5 Set the temperature to 200°C (392°F) and cook for about 10–15 minutes until risen and golden. The bases of the teacakes should sound hollow when tapped. Transfer to a wire rack to cool. Serve the teacakes split and buttered or toasted, if liked.

prep + cook time 35 minutes + proving
makes 9 teacakes

ICED CHERRY CUPCAKES

150 g (5 oz) lightly salted butter,
  softened
150 g (5 oz) caster sugar
3 eggs
175 g (6 oz) self-raising flour
75 g (3 oz) dried cherries
150 g (5 oz) icing sugar
4–5 teaspoons lemon juice
12 fresh cherries, to decorate
  (optional)

1 Line a 6-hole cake tray with paper muffin cases.
2 Put the butter, sugar, eggs and flour in a bowl and beat with a hand-held electric whisk until pale and creamy. Gently fold in the dried cherries. Reserving half the mixture for a second batch, spoon the dough into the muffin cases and place on the lower rack of the halogen oven.
3 Set the temperature to 175°C (347°F) and cook for about 15 minutes until risen and just firm to the touch. Leave in the tin for 5 minutes then transfer to a wire rack while you cook the remainder. Leave to cool completely.
4 Mix the icing sugar with enough lemon juice to make a smooth glacé icing that almost holds its shape. Spread over the cakes and decorate each cake with a fresh cherry, if liked.

prep + cook time 45 minutes
makes 12 cupcakes

VANILLA & WHITE CHOCOLATE CUPCAKES

125 g (4 oz) lightly salted butter,
  softened
175 g (6 oz) caster sugar
2 eggs
100 ml (3½ fl oz) milk
1 teaspoon vanilla bean paste
  or extract
25 g (1 oz) plain flour
100 g (3½ oz) self-raising flour

icing
100 g (3½ oz) cream cheese
25 g (1 oz) white chocolate,
  melted
50 g (2 oz) lightly salted butter,
  softened
½ teaspoon vanilla bean paste
  or extract
250 g (8 oz) icing sugar, plus
  extra for dusting
white chocolate curls, to
  decorate

1 Line a 6-hole muffin tray with paper cake cases.
2 Cream together the butter and caster sugar using a hand-held electric whisk until light and fluffy. Beat in one egg, half the milk and the vanilla, then the plain flour. Stir in the remaining egg and milk. Add the self-raising flour, stirring until just combined. Use to fill the cake cases, reserving the excess to make a second batch. Place on the lower rack of the halogen oven.
3 Set the temperature to 200°C (392°F) and cook for 12–18 minutes until risen and just firm to the touch. Leave in the tin for 5 minutes, then transfer to a wire rack while you cook the remaining mixture.
4 Make the icing. Put the cream cheese, chocolate, butter, vanilla and icing sugar in a bowl and beat until smooth and creamy. Spread over the tops of the cakes. Scatter with plenty of white chocolate curls and dust with extra icing sugar to decorate.

prep + cook time 50 minutes
makes 10–12 cupcakes

FROSTED CARROT CAKE

125 ml (4 fl oz) sunflower oil,
plus extra for oiling
125 g (4 oz) light muscovado
sugar
2 eggs
125 g (4 oz) self-raising flour
1 teaspoon ground mixed spice
125 g (4 oz) carrots, coarsely
grated
25 g (1 oz) sultanas

cream cheese frosting
100 g (3½ oz) full-fat cream
cheese
½ teaspoon vanilla extract
75 g (3 oz) icing sugar
finely grated carrot, to decorate

1 Oil an 18 cm (7 inch) square cake tin and line with greaseproof paper. Oil the paper.
2 Whisk together the oil and muscovado sugar to combine, then whisk in the eggs. Sift the flour and mixed spice into the bowl and stir in. Add the carrots and sultanas, and mix well. Pour the mixture into the tin and level the top. Place on the lower rack of the halogen oven.
3 Set the temperature to 175°C (347°F) and cook for about 30 minutes until just firm to the touch. Leave in the tin for 10 minutes, then transfer to a wire rack to cool.
4 Beat together the cream cheese, vanilla and icing sugar to make the frosting. Spread over the cooled cake with a palette knife and decorate wih a little grated carrot. Serve cut into squares.

prep + cook time 50 minutes
makes 9 squares

BLUEBERRY & APPLE SLICE

125 g (4 oz) lightly salted firm
   butter, plus extra for greasing
200 g (7 oz) self-raising flour
175 g (6 oz) caster sugar
2 eggs
2 tablespoons milk
2 crisp dessert apples, peeled,
   cored and thinly sliced
125 g (4 oz) blueberries
clotted cream, to serve

1 Lightly grease a loaf tin that
will fit on the lower rack of the
halogen oven. Line the base
and long sides with a strip of
greaseproof paper and grease
the paper.
2 Cut the butter into small pieces
and put in a food processor or
blender with the flour. Blend
until the mixture resembles fine
breadcrumbs. Add the sugar,
eggs and milk and blend to form
a dough.
3 Spread half the cake mixture
into the loaf tin. Scatter over half
the apples and blueberries and
cover with the remaining cake
mixture. Spread the remaining
fruits over the top, cover with foil
and place on the lower rack of the
halogen oven.
4 Set the temperature to 175°C
(347°F) and cook for 30 minutes.
Remove the foil and cook for
about another 15 minutes or until
a skewer inserted into the centre
comes out clean. Leave in the tin
for 10 minutes, then transfer to a
plate or board. Serve warm with
clotted cream.

prep + cook time about 1 hour
makes 8 slices

PISTACHIO & CHOCOLATE TORTE

50 g (2 oz) unsalted shelled
  pistachio nuts, plus extra
  2 tablespoons, skinned and
  roughly chopped, to decorate
125 g (4 oz) lightly salted butter,
  softened
125 g (4 oz) caster sugar
100 g (3½ oz) self-raising flour
40 g (1½ oz) cocoa powder,
  plus extra for dusting
1½ teaspoons baking powder
2 eggs, beaten
4 tablespoons milk
75 g (3 oz) plain dark or milk
  chocolate, chopped
whipped cream, to serve

1 Grind the pistachio nuts in a food processor. Grease a 20 cm (8 inch) sandwich tin or springform tin. Line the bottom with greaseproof paper.

2 Cream together the butter and sugar until smooth and creamy. Beat in the ground pistachio nuts, flour, cocoa powder, baking powder, eggs and milk. Mix until evenly combined.

3 Pour the mixture into the prepared cake tin and spread in an even layer. Scatter the chocolate pieces and extra chopped pistachio nuts over the top and place on the lower rack of the halogen oven.

4 Set the temperature to 175°C (347°F) and cook for about 25 minutes until the top feels firm to the touch. (A skewer inserted into the centre should come out slightly moist.) Leave to cool in the tin for 10 minutes before transferring to a plate. Dust with extra cocoa powder and serve warm with lightly whipped cream.

prep + cook time 45 minutes
serves 4–6

POACHED PEARS IN GINGER WINE

4 firm dessert pears
1 tablespoon lemon juice
300 ml (½ pint) ginger wine
50 g (2 oz) caster sugar
1 cinnamon stick, halved
vanilla ice cream, to serve

1 Peel the pears, leaving the stalks attached, and brush with the lemon juice to prevent discoloration. Pour the wine into a shallow ovenproof dish and place on the lower rack of the halogen oven.
2 Set the temperature to 250°C (482°F) and cook for about 5 minutes until hot. Stir in the sugar, then carefully add the pears and cinnamon. Reduce the heat to 150°C (302°F) and cook for 25–30 minutes until the pears are tender. (The cooking time will vary slightly depending on the ripeness of the pears.) Turn and baste the pears with the wine a couple of times during cooking.
3 Transfer the pears to small serving dishes and spoon over the syrup. Serve warm with vanilla ice cream.

prep + cook time 50 minutes
serves 4

BANANA PUDDING WITH CHOCOLATE SAUCE

125 g (4 oz) lightly salted butter,
  plus extra for greasing
100 g (3½ oz) caster sugar
2 eggs
100 g (3½ oz) self-raising flour
½ teaspoon baking powder
2 tablespoons cocoa powder,
  plus extra for dusting
2 ripe bananas
100 g (3½ oz) plain dark
  chocolate, chopped
2 tablespoons milk
2 tablespoons golden syrup

1 Lightly grease a shallow pie dish. Put 100 g (3½ oz) of the butter, the sugar, eggs, flour, baking powder and cocoa powder in a bowl and beat with a hand-held electric whisk until smooth. Slice the bananas into the bowl and stir in gently. Turn into the prepared dish, cover with foil and place on the lower rack of the halogen oven.

2 Set the temperature to 150°C (302°F) and cook for about 30 minutes or until the pudding is just firm to the touch. Cover the pudding with foil if the top begins to turn brown.

3 Meanwhile, put the chocolate in a small saucepan on the hob with the remaining butter and the milk and golden syrup. Heat gently until the chocolate has melted to form a smooth, glossy sauce.

4 Dust the pudding with cocoa powder and serve with the chocolate sauce.

prep + cook time about 50 minutes
serves 4

CHERRY CLAFOUTIS

50 g (2 oz) unsalted butter
675 g (1 lb 6 oz) pitted black or
  red cherries
4 tablespoons plain flour
75 g (3 oz) caster sugar
3 eggs, beaten
450 ml (¾ pint) milk
vanilla sugar, for dusting

1 Use half the butter to grease the sides of a shallow ovenproof dish. Tip in the cherries and spread into an even layer across the bottom of the dish.

2 Put the flour in a bowl with the sugar. Gradually beat in the eggs to make a smooth batter.

3 Heat the milk in a saucepan on the hob until hot but not boiling and pour over the egg mixture, whisking well. Pour the batter over the cherries and dot with the remaining butter. Cover the dish with foil and place on the top rack of the halogen oven.

4 Set the temperature to 165°C (329°F) and cook for about 30 minutes until the batter is only lightly set in the centre. Uncover the dish and cook for a further 15–20 minutes until the top is firm and golden. Leave to cool slightly before serving, dusted with vanilla sugar.

prep + cook time about 1 hour
serves 6

CLASSIC RICE PUDDING

50 g (2 oz) unsalted butter, plus
　extra for greasing
150 g (5 oz) pudding rice
150 g (5 oz) caster sugar
1.3 litres (2¼ pints) milk
2 bay leaves
plenty of freshly grated nutmeg

1 Butter the sides of a large ovenproof dish. Put the rice, sugar, milk and bay leaves into the dish. (The mixture should come no higher than three-quarters up the dish as it will rise a little as it cooks.) Place on the lower rack of the halogen oven.

2 Set the temperature at 150°C (302°F) and cook for 1 hour, stirring occasionally. Dot with the butter and sprinkle with plenty of freshly grated nutmeg. Cook for a further 1 hour or until the rice is tender. Leave to stand for 15 minutes before serving.

prep + cook time about 2 hours + standing time
serves 6

HONEYED BREAD & BUTTER PUDDING

50 g (2 oz) unsalted butter, softened, plus extra for greasing
4 thin slices good-quality white bread
100 g (3½ oz) raisins
2 eggs
1 egg yolk
finely grated rind of 1 lemon
275 ml (9 fl oz) full-cream or semi-skimmed milk
25 g (1 oz) caster sugar
3 tablespoons clear honey, plus extra to serve (optional)
freshly grated nutmeg

1 Butter the slices of bread generously with the softened butter and cut into triangles. Grease a shallow pie dish and arrange the bread slices in the dish, sprinkling the layers with the raisins.

2 Beat together the eggs and egg yolk in a jug. Whisk in the lemon rind, milk, sugar and honey. Pour the custard over the bread and leave to stand for 1 hour.

3 Sprinkle the top of the pudding with plenty of freshly grated nutmeg. Place the pie on the lower rack of the halogen oven.

4 Set the temperature to 150°C (302°F) and cook the pudding for 35–40 minutes until the top is golden and the custard lightly set. If needed, cover the pudding with foil if the top starts to brown too much. Drizzle with extra honey, if liked, and serve warm with pouring cream.

prep + cook time 55 minutes + standing time
serves 4

CINNAMON APPLE CRUNCH

1 kg (2 lb) cooking apples
75 g (3 oz) caster sugar
1 tablespoon lemon juice
100 g (3½ oz) unsalted butter
1 teaspoon ground cinnamon
200 g (7 oz) porridge oats
50 g (2 oz) light muscovado sugar
vanilla ice cream, to serve

1 Peel, core and slice the apples, then scatter over the bottom of a shallow ovenproof dish and sprinkle with the caster sugar. Drizzle with the lemon juice.

2 Melt the butter in a saucepan on the hob and stir in the cinnamon, then the oats and muscovado sugar until evenly mixed. Spoon the mixture over the apples. Cover the dish with foil and place on the lower rack of the halogen oven.

3 Set the temperature to 200°C (392°F) and cook for 40 minutes, removing the foil for the final 10 minutes of cooking time to colour the crumble topping. Serve with vanilla ice cream.

prep + cook time 1 hour
serves 6

GLOSSARY

basil an aromatic herb; there are many types, but the most commonly used is sweet basil.

bay leaves aromatic leaves from the bay tree available fresh or dried; used to add a strong, slightly peppery flavour to soups, stocks and casseroles.

black olive tapenade a rich soft paste made from black olives, capers and anchovies.

capers the grey-green buds of a warm climate shrub sold either dried and salted or pickled in vinegar brine.

cardamom can be bought in pod, seed or ground form. Has a distinctive, aromatic, sweetly rich flavour.

cayenne pepper thin-fleshed, long, very-hot red chilli; usually purchased dried and ground.

celery salt a flavored salt made from the ground seeds of celery or its relative lovage; used as a food seasoning.

cheese
cream a soft cow-milk cheese with a fat content ranging from 14 per cent to 33 per cent.
gorgonzola an Italian blue cheese, made from unskimmed cow's and/or goat's milk. It can be quite salty, firm or crumbly and has a 'bite'.
haloumi a firm, cream-coloured sheep's milk cheese matured in brine; can be grilled or fried,

briefly, without breaking down.
parmesan a sharp-tasting, dry, hard cheese, made from skimmed or semi-skimmed milk and aged for at least a year.

chickpeas also called garbanzos, hummus or channa; an irregularly round, sandy-coloured legume.

cinnamon dried inner bark of the shoots of the cinnamon tree. Available as a stick or ground.

coriander fragrant herb, available dried as seeds and a ground powder. Fresh coriander, also known as cilantro or chinese parsley, is a bright-green-leafed herb with a pungent flavour. Ground or seeds must never be used to replace fresh coriander or vice versa. The tastes are completely different.

cornflour also known as cornstarch; used as a thickening agent in cooking.

crème fraîche a mature fermented cream (minimum fat content 35%) having a slightly tangy flavour and velvety rich texture; similar thickness to soured cream.

cumin available both ground and as whole seeds; cumin has a warm, earthy, rather strong flavour.

fennel bulb vegetable, also known as finocchio or anise. Also the name given to dried seeds having a liquorice flavour.

fennel seeds dried seeds with a distinct liquorice flavour.

flageolet beans small, creamy, tender-skinned pale green beans with a delicate flavour.

five-spice powder a fragrant mixture of ground cinnamon, cloves, star anise, sichuan pepper and fennel seeds.

garam masala a blend of spices based on varying proportions of cardamom, cinnamon, cloves, coriander, fennel and cumin, roasted and ground together. Black pepper and chilli can be added for a hotter version.

haricot beans small, white, oval beans with a smooth texture and bland in flavour. Haricot beans require soaking.

mint an aromatic herb with a sweet, fresh flavour and a cool aftertaste. Fresh mint is usually preferred in cooking over the dried version.

mixed spice a blend of ground spices usually consisting of cinnamon, allspice and nutmeg.

muscovado sugar a soft, sticky, dark brown unrefined cane sugar. Its dark colour and rich flavour come from the sugarcane juice left in during the production process.

mustard
french plain mild mustard.
powder (dry) finely ground white (yellow) mustard seeds.

wholegrain also known as seeded; a French-style coarse-grain mustard made from crushed mustard seeds and Dijon-style French mustard.

nutmeg dried nut of an evergreen tree; available in ground form or you can grate your own with a fine grater.

oregano also known as wild marjoram; has a woody stalk with clumps of tiny, dark green leaves that have a pungent, peppery flavour and are used fresh or dried.

pancetta an Italian salt-cured pork roll, usually cut from the belly; used, chopped, in cooked dishes to add flavours. Bacon can be substituted.

parsley a multi-purpose herb, it can be used as a garnish and flavouring and as a vegetable. It has two main varieties: curly leaf and flatleaf, which has a stronger flavour and tends to be favoured in Mediterranean cooking.

pesto
basil a paste made from fresh basil, oil, garlic, pine nuts and parmesan.
sun-dried tomato similar to basil pesto, but with sun-dried tomatoes replacing the basil.

pimiento a small sweet red pepper.

root ginger also called green or fresh ginger; the thick gnarled root of a tropical plant. Can be kept, peeled, covered with dry sherry in a jar and refrigerated, or frozen in an airtight container.

rosemary a highly aromatic herb, its needle-like leaves are used both fresh and dried to flavour a variety of dishes, especially roast meats and vegetables.

sauces
soy a thin, salty condiment made from fermented soy beans.
sweet chilli a comparatively mild, Thai-type sauce made from red chillies, sugar, garlic and vinegar.
worcestershire a dark-brown spicy sauce used to season meat, gravies and cocktails, and as a condiment.

shallots also called french shallots, golden shallots or eschalots; small, elongated, brown-skinned members of the onion family. They grow in tight clusters similar to garlic.

shrimp paste also known as trasi or blanchan; pungent, preserved, almost solid paste made of salted dried shrimp.

star anise a dried star-shaped pod, the seeds of which taste of aniseed.

suet
beef cooking fat obtained from the area around the kidney and loins. Rarely available in its natural form, it is grated, mixed with flour and sold in packets.
vegetarian made from palm oil and rice flour, vegetarian suet gives slightly different results to the beef variety.

sun-dried tomato paste concentrated purée made from sun-dried tomatoes and oil; used to flavour soups, stews, sauces and casseroles.

thyme a member of the mint family; has tiny grey-green leaves that give off a pungent minty, light-lemon aroma. Dried thyme comes in both leaf and powdered form.

turmeric a member of the ginger family, its root is dried and ground; intensely pungent in taste but not hot.

vanilla
bean dried long, thin pod from a tropical golden orchid grown in central and South America and Tahiti; the minuscule black seeds inside the bean are used to impart a distinctively sweet vanilla flavour.
extract obtained from vanilla beans infused in water; a non-alcoholic version of essence.
paste an intensely flavoured paste made from a high concentration of vanilla seeds.

vinegar
red wine based on fermented red wine.
white wine based on fermented white wine.

INDEX

CONVERSION CHARTS

weights

METRIC	IMPERIAL
5 g	¼ oz
15 g	½ oz
20 g	¾ oz
25 g	1 oz
50 g	2 oz
65 g	2½ oz
75 g	3 oz
125 g	4 oz
150 g	5 oz
175 g	6 oz
200 g	7 oz
250 g	8 oz
275 g	9 oz
300 g	10 oz
325 g	11 oz
375 g	12 oz
400 g	13 oz
425 g	14 oz
450 g	14½ oz
475 g	15 oz
500 g	1 lb
625 g	1¼ lb
750 g	1½ lb
875 g	1¾ lb
1 kg	2 lb
1.25 kg	2½ lb
1.5 kg	3 lb
1.75 kg	3½ lb
2 kg	4 lb

measurements

METRIC	IMPERIAL
2.5 mm	⅛ inch
5 mm	¼ inch
1 cm	½ inch
1.5 cm	¾ inch
2.5 cm	1 inch
3.5 cm	1½ inches
5 cm	2 inches
6 cm	2½ inches
7 cm	3 inches
10 cm	4 inches
12 cm	5 inches
15 cm	6 inches
18 cm	7 inches
20 cm	8 inches
23 cm	9 inches
25 cm	10 inches
28 cm	11 inches
30 cm	12 inches
33 cm	13 inches

teaspoons

DRY	
1 tsp	5 g
1 tbsp	15 g

LIQUID	
1 tsp	5 ml
1 tbsp	15 ml

liquids

METRIC	IMPERIAL
15 ml	½ fl oz
25 ml	1 fl oz
50 ml	2 fl oz
75 ml	3 fl oz
10 ml	3½ fl oz
125 ml	4 fl oz
150 ml	¼ pint
175 ml	6 fl oz
200 ml	7 fl oz
250 ml	8 fl oz
275 ml	9 fl oz
300 ml	½ pint
325 ml	11 fl oz
350 ml	12 fl oz
375 ml	13 fl oz
400 ml	14 fl oz
450 ml	¾ pint
475 ml	16 fl oz
500 ml	17 fl oz
575 ml	18 fl oz
600 ml	1 pint
750 ml	1¼ pints
900 ml	1½ pints
1 litre	1¾ pints
1.2 litres	2 pints
1.5 litres	2½ pints
1.8 litres	3 pints
2 litres	3½ pints
2.5 litres	4 pints
2.75 litres	5 pints
3.6 litres	6 pints